THE BEATITUDES
AND OTHER MEDITATIONS

By Edward F. Mannino

WingSpan Press

Copyright © 2022 by Edward F. Mannino
All rights reserved.

No part of this book may be reproduced or transmitted in any form or by any means, electronic or mechanical, including photocopying, recording or by any information storage and retrieval system, without written permission from the author, except for the inclusion of brief quotations in review.

Published in the United States and the United Kingdom by WingSpan Press, Livermore, CA

The WingSpan name, logo and colophon are the trademarks of WingSpan Publishing.

ISBN 978-1-63683-032-2 (pbk.)
ISBN 978-1-63683-975-2 (ebk.)

First edition 2022

Printed in the United States of America

www.wingspanpress.com

Front Cover: The Sermon on the Mount by Carl Heinrich Bloch (Public domain)

"Do not conform yourself to this age
But be transformed by the renewal of your mind that you may discern what is the will of God what is good and pleasing and perfect"

ROMANS 12:2

CONTENTS

Preface v
1. The Beatitudes - Poverty Of Spirit 1
2. The Beatitudes - Mourning 3
3. The Beatitudes - Meekness 4
4. The Beatitudes - Hunger For Justice 6
5. The Beatitudes - Mercy 7
6. The Beatitudes - Purity Of Heart 9
7. The Beatitudes - Peacemaking 10
8. The Beatitudes - Persecution 12
9. Catholicism As A Religion Of Paradox 15
10. The Priority Of Christ 17
11. An Advent Meditation 19
12. Ask 21
13. Fasting 23
14. Elijah And The Lesson Of Silence 25
15. Pelagians All? 27
16. The Necessity Of Praise 29
17. Pride 31
18. Riches, Honor, Pride 33
19. Keep It Simple 35
20. Unity 37
21. Faith 39
22. The Spring Of Life 41
23. Repentance: A Lenten Meditation 43
24. The Kingdom Of God 45

25.	"Because Of The Crowd"	47
26.	"Their Hearts Were Hardened"	49
27.	The Paralytic And His Friends	51
28.	The Corporal Works Of Mercy	53
29.	Know, Love, And Serve	57
30.	Christ As Light	59
31.	An Expanded Doxology	61
About The Author		63

PREFACE

The purpose of these meditations is to help us to deepen our faith and to translate it into action. They are designed to help us incorporate the petition of one of my favorite hymns from Midday Prayer in the Liturgy of the Hours. That petition asks "Help us, O Lord, to live/The faith which we proclaim,/That all our thoughts and words and deeds/ May glorify your name."

These meditations can be used in several ways. The design is for a month of reflection on how our faith can influence our life in accord with the teachings of the Gospels. But please use them as best fits your life. But, in any event, please use and reflect upon them.

THE BEATITUDES

The Beatitudes provide a short course in the teachings of the Gospels. They are incorporated in the spiritual lives of the members of many religious Orders and in those of many lay individuals. For example, the Knights and Dames of the Order of Malta wear an eight-pointed Cross on their robes and capes. The Cross symbolizes the Order and represents the eight Beatitudes, which are found in the Gospel of Saint Matthew, at 5:3-10.

Each Beatitude begins with the words "Blessed are.." The Greek word in Matthew's Gospel which is translated as "Blessed" also carries the meaning "Happy." Thus, the Beatitudes, the words of Christ who is the Way, the Truth, and the Life, illuminate the narrow gate to happiness.

Here are some reflections on each beatitude:

The first beatitude: "Blessed are the poor in spirit, for theirs is the Kingdom of Heaven." (Matt. 5:3)

Five spiritual writers afford us great insights into the application of this beatitude to our daily lives.

In his book, *Catholicism: A Journey to the Heart of*

the Faith, Bishop Robert Barron has explained that this beatitude "is neither a romanticizing of economic poverty nor a demonization of wealth, but rather a formula for detachment." (page 43) Thus, the focus is not upon one's wealth or poverty, but rather upon how one views whatever that individual has, and what he or she does with it.

Pope Saint Leo the Great similarly observed in his sermon "On the Beatitudes," that "It is undoubtedly true that the poor achieve humility more readily than the rich; the former may develop a loving meekness, the latter an arrogant spirit. Yet many rich people become humble, for they use their wealth, not to feed their own pride, but to help their neighbors, and count it a great gain to be able to relieve the needs of others.... The blessing falls, then, on the poverty that is not fascinated by love of earthly things and does not yearn for further worldly goods, but desires only to be enriched with the good things of heaven."

Bishop Fulton Sheen, in his book, *The Cross and the Beatitudes*, explains that "The poor in spirit are those who are so detached from wealth, from social position, and from earthly knowledge that, at the moment the Kingdom of God demands a sacrifice, they are prepared to surrender all." (page 37) Father Adrian Van Kaam calls this type of detachment "self alienation," which is separation from our ego-driven desires. *Dynamics of Spiritual Self Direction*, 179-200.

Finally, Brennan Manning interprets this beatitude in terms of our self consciousness of sin: "Blessed are you who are conscious of your lack of merit and readily open yourselves to the divine mercy." *Reflections for Ragamuffins*, 177.

In meditating on this beatitude, we should attempt to identify anything to which we are unduly attached, and which interferes with our ability to lead a holy life.

The second beatitude: "Blessed are they who mourn, for they will be comforted." (Matt. 5:4)

This beatitude includes, but extends our vision far beyond, our usual focus on mourning for a loved one, or for the loss of something we highly valued, such as a friendship.

To begin with, the second beatitude includes mourning for our own personal sinfulness. Saint Paul "rejoices" in his Second Letter to the Corinthians "not because you were saddened, but because you were saddened into repentance." (2 Cor. 7:9) Pope Benedict XVI similarly reminds us that "there is… the mourning occasioned by the shattering encounter with truth, which leads man to undergo conversion and to resist evil. This mourning heals, because it teaches man to hope and to live again." *Jesus of Nazareth*, 86.

Second, this beatitude focussed on mourning also includes mourning for the sins of the culture in which we live, and the sins of our neighbors. Chromatius, a friend of St. Jerome, instructs us that "The blessed of whom he speaks are not those bereaving the death of a spouse....Rather, he is speaking of those blessed persons who…do not cease to mourn over the iniquity of the world or the offenses of sinners with a pious, duty-bound sentiment." *Tractate on Matthew*, 17.3.1-2.

It would be good, in meditating upon this beatitude, to mourn on each of these levels - for those we have lost, for our many sins, and for the corrosive nature of our current culture.

The third beatitude: "Blessed are the meek, for they will inherit the land." (Matt. 5:5)

Meekness is too often equated with being a pushover, letting the world simply roll over you while you practice submissiveness. Nothing could be further from the truth. Archbishop Sheen has said that "meekness is not a spineless passivity which allows everyone to walk over us. No! Meekness is self-possession…A weak man can never be meek, because he is never self-possessed; meekness is the virtue that controls the combative, violent, and pugnacious powers of our nature, and is therefore the best and noblest road to self-realization." *The Cross and the Beatitudes*, 5. Bishop Barron further extends this view, stating that to be meek is to be "free from the addiction to ordinary power." *Catholicism*, 44.

Christ himself is the paragon of meekness. He describes Himself as "meek and humble of heart." (Matt. 11:29) But, as C.S. Lewis put it, "Aslan," his Lion-Christ figure from the *Narnia* stories, "is not a tame lion." Indeed, heaven cannot be reached passively, for "the kingdom of heaven suffers violence, and the violent are taking it by force." (Matt. 11:12)

George Hunsinger, a Presbyterian minister, emphasizes that the meek will always stand up for what is right. They "will speak out for those who are marginalized and humiliated, those who have no rights or from whom those rights are robbed and taken away," but they also will be careful in doing so. He notes that "For the faithful, the question of when to submit and when to resist is an ongoing task of spiritual discernment." *The Beatitudes*, 30. Moreover, "The meek one is more content to endure an offense than to commit one. For unless one is unafraid of being offended, one cannot be without sin." Anonymous author, *Incomplete Work on Matthew,* Homily 9.

Finally, William Barclay has written that meekness requires submitting to the will of God, accepting the trials which cannot be avoided and which we necessarily experience in the course of our lives. *The Beatitudes for Everyman*, 38.

In reflecting on this beatitude, we need to consider whether we are sufficiently self-possessed to be meek. Or, are we instead concerned with gaining or retaining power of some type?

The fourth beatitude: "Blessed are those who hunger and thirst for righteousness, for they shall be satisfied." (Matt 5:6)

Righteousness is an important concept in the New Testament. The Gospels and Epistles refer to it over 70 times. Webster's defines righteousness as "acting in accord with divine or moral law," and "free from guilt or sin."

Chromatius explains that Jesus "taught that we must seek after righteousness with earnest desire, not with faint hearted energy….He calls those persons blessed who in their search for righteousness virtually burn with passionate longing in their hunger and thirst." *Tractate on Matthew* 17.5.1.

Pope Benedict XVI further explains this beatitude: "The people this Beatitude describes are those who are not content with things as they are and refuse to stifle the restlessness of heart that points man toward something greater and so sets him on the inward journey to reach it – rather like the wise men from the East seeking Jesus, the star that shows the way to truth, to love, to

God. The people meant here are those whose interior sensitivity enables them to see and hear the subtle signs that God sends into the world to break the dictatorship of convention." Jesus of Nazareth, 90.

Saint John Chrysostom states that those who hunger and thirst for righteousness will be satisfied because "it is righteousness that produces true wealth." *The Gospel of Matthew,* Homily 15.4.

While we may desire to attain righteousness, can we truly say that we "hunger and thirst" for it? We should reflect on how strong is our desire for righteousness, and how we can increase our ability to act in accordance with divine law.

The fifth beatitude: "Blessed are the merciful, for they shall obtain mercy." (Matt. 5:7)

Mercy is one of the principal manifestations of God's love for us. As there is no limit to God's mercy, there should be no limit to ours.

The word "mercy" in this beatitude comes from the Latin words meaning a "sorrowful heart." Archbishop Sheen instructs us that "Mercy is…a compassionate understanding of another's unhappiness. A person is merciful when he feels the sorrow and misery of another as if it were his own." *The Cross and the Beatitudes,*

15. The parable of the Good Samaritan vivifies this definition of mercy. Pope Benedict XVI explains that the Good Samaritan, moved by compassion at the sight of the robbers' victim, is "struck in his soul by the lightning flash of mercy." *Jesus of Nazareth*, 177. When we demonstrate such mercy to others, Pope St. Gregory the Great noted that "we bear the Lord's cross…when, out of compassion for our neighbor, we make their afflictions our own."

Our obligation to demonstrate mercy to others does not stop with relatives, friends, or even the victim of the robbers in the parable of the Good Samaritan. One early Christian author puts it this way: "The kind of compassion referred to here is not simply giving alms to the poor or orphan or widow. This kind of compassion is often found even among those who hardly know God. But that person is truly compassionate who shows compassion even to his own enemy and treats the enemy well." Anonymous author, *Incomplete Work on Matthew,* Homily 9.

The fifth beatitude promises that those who practice mercy to others will be rewarded by receiving mercy themselves. Father Benedict Groeschel explains that even the merciful themselves need mercy. This is because "they realize how desperately they need it. If mercy opens your mind and heart to the needs of someone else, it infallibly will teach you how much *you* need mercy." *Heaven in Our Hands*, 108.

Finally, as Shakespeare wrote, the merciful are "twice blest: It blesseth him that gives, and him that takes." *The Merchant of Venice*, Act 4, Scene 1.

In reflecting on the fifth beatitude, we need to consider who are those in our lives who need a demonstration of mercy from us to them.

The sixth beatitude: "Blessed are the pure in heart, for they shall see God." (Matt. 5:8)

Pope Benedict XVI explains that "The pure heart is the loving heart that enters into communion of service and obedience with Jesus Christ." *Jesus of Nazareth*, 95. In a similar fashion, Archbishop Sheen states that "Purity… is surrender, it is thoughtfulness of others, it is sacrifice." *The Cross and the Beatitudes*, 33.

The pure of heart are steadfast in their beliefs and actions. If we are pure in heart, Bishop Barron explains that there is "no ambiguity in your heart…about what is important."

Two early Christian commentators give further insight into this beatitude. St. John Chrysostom states that "Those he here calls pure are either those who have so fully filled their lives with goodness that they are practically unaware of evil within themselves, or he may be referring to those who live a moderate, simple life, [f]or there is nothing that we need so much in order to behold God as a self-controlled life." *The Gospel of Matthew*, Homily 15.4. Chromatius assures us that the pure in heart are "those who, living by faith in God with a pure mind and unstained conscience, will win the right to see the God of glory in the heavenly kingdom to come." *Tractate on Matthew*, 17.6.3-4.

Finally, Father Groeschel cautions us that purity in heart "is not a static condition, an ultimate goal at which we can never arrive in this life. Rather, it is something for which we constantly labor." *Heaven in Our Hands*, 17.

As we reflect on this beatitude, we should consider what concrete steps we can take in our journey toward approaching purity in heart, including how we can better serve others.

The seventh beatitude: "Blessed are the peacemakers, for they shall be called children of God." (Matt. 5:9)

The peace of which this beatitude speaks goes beyond the negative of suppression of hostility or aggression among people. Instead, peacemakers are called to spread the peace of Christ. In the Gospel of John, Jesus promises and explains: "Peace I leave with you; *my peace* I give to you. Not as the world gives do I give it to you." John 14:27. This peace is that signified by the Hebrew word, "Shalom," which "signifies harmonious friendship, covenant intimacy, a relationship of trust." Edward Sri, *Praying the Rosary Like Never Before*, 127.

Paul further explains that this peace is based upon reconciliation of all things through Christ, who "reconcile[s] all things for him, making peace by the blood of his cross." *Colossians* 1:20.

Pope Benedict XVI notes that this peace "applies first of all in the context of each person's life," and that "Only the man who is reconciled with God can also be reconciled and in harmony with himself, and only the man who is reconciled with God and with himself can establish peace around him and throughout the world." *Jesus of Nazareth*, 85.

Finally, Bishop Barron explains that "someone who has ordered himself fundamentally toward God is...a peacemaker, for he will necessarily channel the metaphysical energy that draws things and people together. One of the most readily recognizable marks of sanctity - on clear display in all the saints - is just this radiation of reconciling power." *Catholicism*, 42.

As we meditate on this beatitude, we should reflect on how we can, with God's help, instill harmony within ourselves, so that we can be reconciled with ourselves and with God, and thus radiate peace to the others in our lives.

The eighth beatitude: "Blessed are those who are persecuted for righteousness sake, for theirs is the kingdom of heaven." (Matt. 5:10)

This last beatitude is particularly timely in our current conditions. People of faith are subjected to an increasingly hostile environment. They are martyred or imprisoned in many places across the globe. In our own country, we are subjected to lawsuits, fines, and shuttering of our businesses for failing to follow mandates which require engaging in practices contrary to our faith.

This is nothing new in history of religion. The early Christians suffered gruesome martyrdoms and, before them, the Jewish people were persecuted to renounce their religion by foreign conquerors who invaded their country. While many people, Jews and Christians, did renounce their religion to avoid death, we read in Chapter 7 of the second book of Maccabees of the inspiring martyrdom of a mother and her seven sons who refused to bow down to the dictates of foreign gods. They stand even today as "a sign of contradiction" (Luke 2:34) to the ways of what Saint Augustine called "the city of man."

Bishop Barron points out that this beatitude "gets in the way of the addictive attachment to honor." He explains that "Many people who are not terribly attracted to wealth, pleasure, or power are held captive by their desire for the approval of others, and they will, accordingly, order their lives, arrange their work, and plot their careers with the single value in mind of being noticed, honored, and endowed with titles." *Catholicism*, 44-45.

Pope Benedict XVI explains that "righteousness" as it is used in this beatitude refers to fidelity to the word of God, and that such fidelity requires "nonconformity with evil," that is, those "existing models of behavior that the individual is pressured to accept because 'everyone does it'." People will be persecuted for resisting evil because "faith will always appear as a contradiction to the 'world' – to the ruling powers at any given time. For this reason, there will be persecution for the sake of righteousness in every period of history." *Jesus of Nazareth*, 87-89.

In our own country today, Archbishop Chaput reminds us that "if we're true to the Catholic faith, people will try to silence us. They'll work to force us out of the public square. They'll press us to compromise on our moral convictions." *Strangers in a Strange Land*, 182.

As we reflect during this month on the last beatitude, we should ask ourselves whether our desire for collegiality at work and in other groups, or our quest for professional honors, tempts us to water down our faith in practice. The beatitudes urge us not to do so. As Archbishop Chaput observes, the beatitudes "teach us that true happiness is union with God, and that the path to happiness is one of poverty of spirit, meekness, hunger, mercy, purity, peace, and courageous witness. They offer us a grand adventure. It's ours to accept or refuse." *Strangers in a Strange Land*, 184.

CATHOLICISM AS A RELIGION OF PARADOX

In his excellent book, *That Nothing May Be Lost*, Father Paul Scalia devotes a 20 page chapter to "Paradoxes of Faith." Among many other examples, he points out that, as Catholics, we believe that Christ is both human and divine, that Mary is both Virgin and mother, and that it is the publican, not the Pharisee, who is "at right with God." (Luke 18:9-14) We also believe that "Whoever loves his life loses it, and whoever hates his life in this world will preserve it for eternal life." (John 12:25) And we "proclaim Christ crucified, a stumbling block to Jews and foolishness to Gentiles…for the foolishness of God is wiser than a human wisdom, and the weakness of God is stronger than human strength."(1 Cor. 1:22,25)

What are we to make of these paradoxes? What do we learn from this approach to teaching our Faith?

While our religion is rooted in reason, human reason and learning are not sufficient. Paradoxes teach us that there is something more, something that reason alone cannot unpack. As Pascal put it, "the heart has its reasons of which reason knows nothing. We know the truth not only by the reason, by the heart." The something more that paradoxes reveal is Faith. As Saint Anselm explained, "I do not seek to understand in order to believe, but I believe in order to understand." Paradoxes challenge us to confront the reality that Faith precedes understanding.

THE PRIORITY OF CHRIST

The Priority of Christ is the name of one of Bishop Robert Barron's first books. The message of that book is that "a densely textured, detailed picture of Jesus becomes the permanent point of reference" for each Christian. Pope Benedict XVI similarly reminds us that "Being Christian is not the result of an ethical choice or a lofty idea, but the encounter with an event, a person, which gives life a new horizon and a decisive direction." That encounter is one with the person of Jesus Christ, Who is "the Way, the Truth, and the Life." (John 14:6) It is through this encounter that we learn to model our life on Him.

By focusing on the person of Christ, we prevent Christianity from becoming a recipe religion, one which simply mandates that its followers adopt particular beliefs and practices. Instead of beginning with such an abstract list of dos and don'ts, we *absorb* the appropriate behaviors by modeling our lives on the lived reality of Christ's actual life, as narrated in the Gospels.

Such an approach incorporates the best manner of learning. When, for example, a young person learns to play baseball, he or she does not do so by reading a baseball rule book, but rather by watching a parent or coach demonstrate how to play the game.

The Beatitudes and Other Meditations

To lead a good Christian life, we must return to the source — Jesus Christ.

AN ADVENT MEDITATION

Advent (Latin for "coming") is a time of expectant joy. Like small children on Christmas Eve savoring the expectation of the coming presents to be brought to them by Santa, we should be thankful for the present of the birth of our Savior, Jesus Christ.

Bishop Robert Barron draws our attention to the Advent hymn, "O Come, Emmanuel," reminding us that the purpose of Christ coming is to "ransom captive Israel." We, too, are captives as well — captives to sin. If we are to be ransomed, we must prepare. When a guest is to come to your house, you get your house in order. Advent is the season for us to do so as well. Thus, Father Alfred Delp, who was executed by the Nazis, described Advent as the season in which to "awaken," a season in which to "place things again in the order that they were given by God the Lord."

How can we get our house in order? A thorough examination of conscience, followed by a sincere sacramental confession, is a wonderful first step. Reading and reflecting on the Scriptures on daily basis, and attending Mass frequently during Advent, are additional salutary ways to prepare for the coming of our Savior, Jesus Christ.

ASK

"ASK" is salvation's acronym.

A = Ask
Pray the *Anima* Christi, and **Ask** Christ to hide you in His wounds, to sanctify you, to save you, to inebriate you, to wash you, and to strengthen you.

S = Seek
Look everywhere for the presence of God about and within you — **Seek** Him in those you love, in those you meet or see, in creation, in your work, in what you read or watch, and in your innermost thoughts and desires.

K = Knock
If you wish to possess a closer relationship with Christ, **Knock** at His door. He will let you in, but you first have to walk to the door and knock.

"For the one who asks always receives; the one who searches always finds; the one who knocks will always have the door opened to him." Matthew 7:8 (Jerusalem Bible).

We must not only speak (ask); we must also take action (seek and knock).

FASTING

In addition to prayer and almsgiving, one of the three pillars of Lent is fasting. By fasting from food and abstaining from meat, we discipline our bodies to recognize our utter dependency on God for our continued existence. The Eastern Orthodox Metropolitan Kallistos Ware tells us that the purpose of fasting is "to lead us in turn to a sense of inward brokenness and contrition."

But there is another, equally important aspect of fasting. Ware gives us insights on this aspect of fasting from two great saints. To begin with, St. John Chrysostom reminds us that we must fast "not only from food but from sins." Next, St. Basil brings the point much closer to home by applying it to criticism of other people. He states that by engaging in slander, "You do not eat meat, but you devour your brother and sister."

In Isaiah 58:6-7, the Lord explains that the fasting He wishes is "releasing those bound unjustly; untying the thongs of the yoke; Setting free the oppressed, breaking every yoke; Sharing your bread with the hungry, sheltering the oppressed and the homeless; Clothing the naked when you see them, and not turning your back on your own."

The Lenten Season gives us each the opportunity to

take a variety of other affirmative steps to assist others, and in that way to serve our neighbors, and fast from the sin of self absorption.

See Kallistos Ware, "The Meaning of the Great Fast," *The Lenten Triodion*. The quotations above from this book are reprinted in *The Glenstal Book of Readings for the Seasons*, at 124-127.

ELIJAH AND THE LESSON OF SILENCE

Under sentence of death from Jezebel for his defeat and destruction of the priests of the pagan god Baal, the prophet Elijah flees to the wilderness. Imploring God to take his life, Elijah is told instead to journey to Mount Horeb, retracing the steps of the Exodus and of Moses. Fasting for 40 days like Moses, Elijah is told by God to wait on the mountain for Him to pass by. 1 *Kings* 19.

Elijah waits, and hears in succession the loud sounds of wind, earthquake, and fire — the same signs Moses experienced before the Ten Commandments were given to him on the same mountain, and that Mary and the Apostles witnessed at Pentecost. But God is not in the wind, the earthquake, or the fire. Instead, Elijah experiences sheer silence, which he understands is the presence of God.

Cardinal Robert Sarah has the same insight. He has written that "silence is where God dwells. He drapes himself in silence." *The Power of Silence: Against the Dictatorship of Noise*, at 30.

Enzo Bianchi, prior of the ecumenical monastic community of Bose, in Italy, tells us that "God is an abyss of silence," and that Elijah's experience of God teaches us that "to listen to God's voice, silence and calm are required; it is necessary to quiet interior noise." (*God: where are you?*, at 103, 105). Bianchi warns that

"When believers blame God for being mute when we attribute to him the emptiness of our own heart, this is… due to our inability to listen, because we seek from him a word that is in our own image and likeness. " (Id. at 106).

Learning to quiet our lives, and simply to listen, is the lesson of Elijah.

PELAGIANS ALL?

Pelagius was a British theologian of the fifth century. His teaching, as refined by his disciple Celestius, was that original sin was not inherited, and that humans are therefore able to choose good by their own nature. With the support of St. Augustine, the Pelagian doctrine was condemned as heretical at the Council of Ephesus in 431.

The Congregation for the Doctrine of Faith has identified a modern version of "neo- Pelagianism," under which the "radically autonomous" individual "presumes to save oneself" and sees salvation as depending upon "the strength of the individual or on purely human structures." *Placuit Deo* (February 22, 2018).

Many of us can be viewed as neo-Pelagians because we think we can combat sin and evil in individual battle, relying solely on our personal strength of will to defeat them. This is why we so regularly fail, and repeatedly fall into the same sins.

Instead of relying on our individual autonomous efforts, we must recognize with the CDF that "salvation consists in our union with Christ," and "incorporating ourselves into His life," since He is The Way. This is why the Psalms repeatedly characterize God as a stronghold, a rock, a refuge, and a shelter of protection. In short, we cannot save ourselves by individual effort alone.

THE NECESSITY OF PRAISE

One of the pervasive themes of the Psalms is the individual's need always to praise God. We see this in Psalm 95, with which the Liturgy of the Hours begins the day's prayers as "a morning invitation to prayer." We read "Come, ring out our joy to the Lord; hail the rock who saves us." Similarly, Psalm 150, the last psalm, employs the word praise 11 times in 7 verses, ending with the exhortation "Let everything that lives and breaths give praise to the Lord. Alleluia." Psalm 100, an alternative invitatory psalm in the Liturgy of the Hours, tells us to "Enter his courts with songs of praise. Give thanks to him and bless his name." This Psalm is immortalized in the hymn, "Praise God, From Whom All Blessings Flow."

The Psalms have another message for our prayer. They also repeatedly describe God as a "refuge," as a "rescuer," as a "helper close at hand, in time of distress," and as a "strength." See, for example, Psalms 30, v. 2; Psalm 39, v. 18; and Psalm 45, v. 2. While we often pray to God for help in accordance with these psalms, we too frequently forget the earlier psalms' reminder to praise Him.

As the Liturgy of the Hours demonstrates, it is fitting to begin each day praising our Creator and Redeemer.

PRIDE

"Pride," the Book of Sirach tells us, "is the reservoir of sin, a source which runs over with vice." (Sirach 10:13) It is the great sin for it draws us inward, making us a prisoner of our ego. It prevents us from serving our neighbor in charity, and it is the gateway sin to other sins.

The temptation to pride is especially dangerous in our current culture, which Pope Benedict XVII accurately described as one of "exaggerated individualism." The focus today is too often inward, with so many believing that they are the masters of their selves, even to the extent of claiming to change their gender. This culture has rightly been termed a "culture of self-invention."

The solution to this exaggerated individualism is humility, by which the sense of self is subliminated. The French philosopher and mystic, Simone Weil, described humility as "the refusal to exist outside God," necessitating a "consent to withdraw [from self] in order to make room for him."

Finally, the Gospels tell us that the kingdom of heaven belongs to those who are like children. (Matthew 19:13-15). As Bishop Barron explains, children "haven't yet learned how to look at themselves." In practicing humility, we seek to escape from our ego, and reach out to other people.

RICHES, HONOR, PRIDE

In the second week of his *Spiritual Exercises*, Saint Ignatius Loyola counsels us to meditate on the standards set forth by Christ, and to compare those standards to those set forth by Lucifer.

Ignatius tells us that Lucifer holds out, as "traps and chains," three things - riches, honor, and pride, and "from these three steps the enemy leads people on to every other vice."

Consider, for example, a self-made business person. He or she strives to attain business success, which is equated with monetary riches. Having obtained the riches, they yearn for something more. They begin to fund charitable causes, and may even pay for a construction of a building (named after them, of course) at a prestigious university, or contribute to an organization which in turn confers upon them its signature honor. At that point, our business person swells up with pride, concluding that he or she has reached the pinnacle of success. But all of these people soon find that riches, honor, and pride do not lead to satisfaction or happiness.

Now consider what Christ sets forth as standards. Instead of riches, He counsels poverty of spirit, since riches require hoarding and constant attention to the exclusion of what is important. Instead of honor, Christ points to persecution, because those who strive to uphold His traditional values are ridiculed by the same organizations which award those honors to those who embrace their secular values. Instead of pride, Christ calls for humility, following in His steps, becoming "meek and humble of heart." (Matthew 11:29) To follow Christ's standards leads to being "Blessed" - the word repeatedly used in the Beatitudes - which means "happy."

Obtaining riches, honor, and glory do not result in such blessedness. We each need to examine whether we succumb to the lure of riches, honor, or pride at the expense of practicing poverty of spirit, unpopularity, and humility.

KEEP IT SIMPLE

Christ instructs us that "I tell you solemnly unless you change and become like little children, you will never enter the kingdom of heaven" (Matt 18:3) Saint Hilary of Poitiers observes that small children "believe through the faith of listening. For children typically follow their father, love their mother, do not know how to wish ill on their neighbor, show no concern for wealth, are not proud, do not hate, do not lie, believe what has been said and hold what they hear as truth. And when we assume this habit and will in all the emotions, we are shown the passageway to the heavens. We must therefore return to the simplicity of children, because with it we shall embrace the beauty of the Lord's humility."

The virtue of simplicity is manifested in the Blessed Mother's choice to appear to children and to the simple. She chose to appear to the fourteen year old Saint Bernadette at Lourdes, and the three young shepherd children at Fatima. She also chose the devout, but simple, Saint Juan Diego to appear to as Our Lady of Guadalupe in Mexico, and a twenty eight year old farm girl, Adele Brise, to appear to as Our Lady of Good Help in Wisconsin.

Even the most intellectual of theologians recognizes this virtue of simplicity. Near the end of his life, Saint

Thomas Aquinas is reported to have said that "All that I have written appears to be as so much straw after the things that have been revealed to me."

As we go about our lives, we should trust, as a child does, in the providential care of our heavenly Father. "Simplify" must be our watchword.

UNITY

Today we find serious and contentious divisions in our society. While they are most obvious in politics, they range far wider, affecting even the Church. Both the Old and New Testaments denounce such division, and call instead for unity.

Psalm 133:1 proclaims that "How good and pleasant it is, when brothers dwell together as one!" Peter Chrysologus commented on this verse, stating that "For not singularity but unity is acceptable to God. The Holy Spirit descended on the apostles with all his welling fountain when they were assembled together. This occurred after the apostles had been instructed by the Lord's own commandment to wait in a group for the Spirit's coming." (Sermon 132)

The Letters of Saint Paul also call for unity, and criticize division. In a famous passage, Saint Paul compared the unity that should characterize Christians with the unity of the different parts of the body, each different, but all working together. 1 Cor. 12: 12-30. Paul also states that "I urge you, brothers, in the name of our Lord Jesus Christ, that all of you agree in what you say, and that there be no divisions among you, but that you be united in the same mind and in the same purpose." 1 Cor.1:10. Origen of Alexandria underlined this point. He said "Where there are sins, there are multiplicity, schisms, heresies, dissensions. But where there is virtue, there is singleness and union, on the basis of which all believers are one heart and one soul."

We need to keep this in mind in all of our activities. Too often we find Catholics assailing one another, as well as priests, bishops, cardinals, and pope, in harsh and condemnatory language over issues of doctrine, liturgy, and even church architecture. While we can and must, as Saint Paul recognized, defend doctrine on issues such as abortion and sin, we must do so by counseling, not defaming, those with whom we disagree. The Great Hymn, "Faith of Our Fathers," written by Frederick Faber, teaches that we must preach to friend and foe alike "as love knows how/ By kindly deeds and virtuous life."

FAITH

One recurring theme in the Gospels is the necessity for faith. Miraculous cures occur only in people who possess faith in Jesus to cure them. We find faith in the story about the centurion's servant (Matt 8:5-13), where the centurion tells Jesus that He need not come to the centurion's home to heal his servant, but "only say the word and my servant will be healed."

Similarly, in the interwoven stories of Jairus and the woman with the hemorrhage (Mark 5:21-43), faith leads to cures for both Jairus' daughter and the afflicted woman. Jesus makes the link clear, telling the woman "your faith has saved you." Yet another example is found in the story of the paralytic man lowered through the roof to be cured by Jesus. (Mark 2:1-12)

By contrast, lack of faith stands as an obstacle to miraculous cures. Thus, when Jesus preaches in his hometown, people question his powers. (Mark 6:1-6) such that "He was amazed at their lack of faith," and could not "perform any mighty deed there."

Do we have faith in God? Do we trust Him to show mercy to us? How can we increase our faith if it is weak or even nonexistent? One way is to read the New Testament in light of the Old Testament, to see how the prophecies of the Old are realized in the New. The best way to do this is to read and reflect upon a good biblical commentary or the writings of the Fathers. A second way is to reflect on our own lives. The Orthodox Saint, Theophan the Recluse, put it this way: "You will not find a single person who has never in his life experienced some unexpected deliverance from misfortune or some unexpected turn of his life for the better. Revive your soul with recollections of such instances… God will arrange everything for the better now, as He has done before." (St. Theophan the Recluse, *Thoughts for Each Day of the Year*, 278.)

THE SPRING OF LIFE

Many of us are dismayed when we find we are not absorbing as we should what we read in Scripture, or hear proclaimed at church. When we find ourselves in this mindset, we should take comfort from a commentary by St. Ephrem, the deacon. Ephrem was a theologian and poet of the fourth century, living in what is now Syria. He wrote many works honoring Jesus and the Virgin Mary, as well as works defending the Catholic Church. He is known as "The Prophet of the Syrians," and "The Lyre of the Holy Spirit." He was declared a Doctor of the Church in 1920 by Pope Benedict XV.

Ephrem compared God's words to a living spring. He said "Whenever anyone discovers some part of the treasure, you should not think that he has exhausted God's word. Instead you should feel that this is all that he was able to find of the wealth contained in it." Moreover, "Be glad then that you are overwhelmed, and do not be sad because he has overcome you. A thirsty man is happy when he is drinking, and he is not depressed because he cannot exhaust the spring…Be thankful then for what you have received, and do not be saddened at all that such an abundance still remains. What you have received and attained is your present share, while what is left will be your heritage. For what you could not take at one time because of your weakness, you will be able to grasp at another if you only persevere."

As it is true with so many aspects of our lives, perseverance is the key to retaining and understanding the Scriptures. What we sip today from the spring of God's words, we will drink more fully and quench our thirsts, if we persevere in our scriptural readings.

Note: A longer excerpt from the commentary by St. Ephrem may be found in the Liturgy of the Hours, in the Second Reading from the Office of Readings for the Sixth Sunday in Ordinary Time.

REPENTANCE: A LENTEN MEDITATION

Lent is a good time to pursue personal repentance. At the beginnings of their ministries, both John the Baptist and Jesus emphasized the need for repentance, calling on their listeners to repent. John proclaimed "Repent, for the kingdom of heaven is close at hand." (Matt. 3:2) Jesus announced that "The time has come… and the Kingdom of God is close at hand. Repent, and believe in the Good News." (Mark 1:15; Matt. 4:17).

What is repentance? St. Bernard personalized that concept. He said that "Repentance is the feeling of a man irritated with himself."

What does repentance require? John the Baptist gave the answer when he told the Pharisees, "Bear fruit that befits repentance." (Matt. 3:8). How can we do that? Great guidance in bearing the fruit of repentance is found in both the Beatitudes and in the Corporal and Spiritual Works of Mercy. The Beatitudes have been discussed in Meditations1 through 8. The Works of Mercy are discussed later, and can be summarized in three components: Help others, Teach others, and Forgive others.

We are called to repentance throughout our lives, and a wonderful way to start on the path to repentance is to practice daily the Beatitudes and the Works of Mercy.

The Beatitudes and Other Meditations

As Mother Teresa put it, "Go out into the world today and love the people you meet. Let your presence light new light in the hearts of people."

THE KINGDOM OF GOD

In the first chapter of Mark's Gospel, we are told that "the kingdom of God is at hand. Repent, and believe in the gospel." (Mark 1:15) The reference to "the kingdom of God" has caused confusion to many. What is the kingdom of God and where is it? Jesus told the Pharisees that "behold, the kingdom of God is in the midst of you." (Luke 17:21, RSV translation) On the most obvious level, this refers to the presence of Jesus himself among the Pharisees. Another translation of this passage in Luke's Gospel places the kingdom of God "within you." This invites us to look within ourselves to find Christ. A prayer to the Sacred Heart invites us "to recall often today your presence in my heart and soul."

St. John Damascene interpreted this passage to teach that "When our outward senses are still and we rejoice in the presence of God within us and retire from the noise and troubles of this world, then we see the kingdom of God within us." (Quoted in *The Navarre Bible: New Testament*, at 322) Saint Paul similarly observed that "For the kingdom of God it is not food and drink, but righteousness and peace and joy in the Holy Spirit." (Romans 14:17)

The word "repent" echoes the same thought. It calls for a change of vision, moving from the selfish claims of the ego to the teachings of the gospels. Bishop Robert

Barron explains that the Greek word translated as "repent" can be translated as "go beyond the mind that you have." This metanoia means trusting in God instead of reacting in fear, and calls us to go inward to find God. *The Word on Fire Bible, The Gospels*, at 185.

"BECAUSE OF THE CROWD"

In two places in the Gospel of Luke, we are told that individuals seeking Jesus were blocked from reaching Him "because of the crowd." In Luke 5:19, friends of a paralytic could not reach Jesus to request that he be cured "because of the crowd," and had to resort to going up to the roof of the house Jesus was in and lowering the paralytic on his stretcher down in front of Jesus. Similarly, in Luke 19:3, Zacchaeus the tax collector, who was "short in stature," could not see Jesus "because of the crowd" and had to climb a tree to see him.

Beyond literal meanings, Sacred Scripture also has what the Church Fathers termed allegory or a "higher vision." In the case of the two passages from the Gospel of Luke, we may interpret them to warn how paying too much attention to what the predominant culture ("the crowd") preaches hides or dilutes the teaching of the Gospels. The influence of "the crowd" is particularly pernicious today where same-sex marriage and transgenderism, among other practices, are lauded as acceptable. To reach Jesus, we must surmount that crowd.

Note: Passages from early Church theologians, including Origen and Clement of Alexandria, which discuss the allegorical and higher vision interpretations of Sacred Scripture are found in *The Christianity Reader* (Mary Gerhart & Fabian Udo, eds.) (2007), at 20-34.

"THEIR HEARTS WERE HARDENED"

In chapter 6 of Mark's Gospel, the Apostles are returning from the mountain where Jesus multiplied the loaves and fishes to feed the 5000. As they row across the sea, they encountered a great wind which tossed them about. They saw Jesus walking on the water, and were terrified because they thought they had seen a ghost. Jesus gets in the boat, and calms the wind, which miracle "astounded" the Apostles.

This account ends with the troubling commentary that "They had not understood the incident of the loaves. On the contrary their hearts were hardened." (Gospel of Mark 6:51-52)

This "hardening of the heart" is the same description that the Book of Exodus gave to the Egyptian Pharaoh when he refused to release the Jewish people from their captivity in Egypt despite the plagues God had visited upon the country. Jesus also accused the Pharisees of the same sin. Why are the Apostles charged with the same deficiency?

Few biblical scholars have attempted to explain this passage. Perhaps it is because the Apostles were not open to the manifestation of God in the miracle of the loaves and fishes even though it was performed in their presence. Inconceivable as that may seem, they failed to grasp its significance.

The Beatitudes and Other Meditations

We should not be too hard on the apostles. Instead we should reflect on how often are guilty of the same hardening of the heart. How often do we fail to see or appreciate the manifestations of God's intervention in our daily lives?

THE PARALYTIC AND HIS FRIENDS

In the Gospel of Mark, 2:1-12, we read the story of the paralytic who could not get into Jesus' presence because of the crowd blocking him from entering the house in which Jesus was ministering to many sick people. In his excellent series, *In Conversation with God*, the Opus Dei priest Father Francis Fernandez Carvajal explains that "the paralytic represents every man who is prevented by sins or his ignorance from reaching God."

The paralytic is saved by his ingenious and loyal friends who carry him to the roof, open it, and lower him down directly before Jesus. These friends have no fear of the crowd's disapproval, refusing to allow any obstacle from hindering them from saving their friend. They represent a model of the successful apostolate, leading their friends or acquaintances who are mired in sin to God.

This parable forces us to consider just to what extent are we willing to go to help our friends be restored to God's saving presence. If our apostolate as to be successful, we must be willing to ignore criticisms so we can serve our friends without fear or hesitation, overcoming whatever obstacles are placed in our path.

The Beatitudes and Other Meditations

The discussion of the paralytic is found in Father Fernandez' *In Conversation with God*, Volume 3, Ordinary Time, at 52.

THE CORPORAL WORKS OF MERCY

The corporal works of mercy provide a handy guide to the obligations that we owe to our fellow humans. By practicing them, we recognize and honor the dignity of every person.

The first two works of mercy call us to feed the hungry and give drink to the thirsty. Many religious and lay groups, including the Knights of Columbus and the Order of Malta, do this literally, feeding the homeless on the street or providing food and drink to them in shelters and churches. Individuals can also practice these works of mercy by preparing food for local aid organizations which feed the poor and homeless, or by contributing to, or volunteering in, homeless shelters, and by providing financial aid to the organizations which help those in need.

The third corporal work of mercy requires us to shelter the homeless. Here, again, financial aid to those organizations which do this is an easy way to help. Volunteering to help in a homeless shelter provides an even more beneficial way to satisfy this obligation. In addition, donating blankets and food for homeless shelters is a helpful work of mercy.

The fourth corporal work of mercy calls us to visit the sick. Too often, even friends of those who fall ill fail to honor this obligation out of fear for their own health or because they are uncomfortable or uncertain as to what to do or say. One such example was provided by a friend of mine who had a colleague dying from ALS who told him that my friend was the only friend who visited him.

The fifth work of mercy calls upon us to visit prisoners. Many parishes or organizations have prison ministries which provide Bibles and other spiritual reading to those incarcerated. Prison visits are also conducted by members of those organizations. Where that is not feasible for us to do so in person, financial aid is always welcome.

The sixth corporal work of mercy is to bury the dead. We do our part here by attending funerals, visiting the bereaved survivors, and providing prayers for the dead, including arranging for Masses to be said for them. Visiting cemeteries to honor those we know who have died and praying for them there is another way to honor this commitment.

The seventh and final corporal work of mercy calls upon us to give alms to the poor. The word "alms" has a Latin root which means "mercy." Giving alms is a work of mercy, and has long been a basic requirement for all, expanded on in both the Old and New Testaments in many books and passages. In Advent, moreover, we are called to engage in prayer, sacrifice and almsgiving. Almsgiving helps the giver as well as the receiver. In Chapter 3 of the book of Sirach, for example, we are told that "Water puts out a blazing fire, almsgiving expiates sin." (Jerusalem Bible translation).

The corporal works of mercy thus provide a helpful guidebook to assist us in practicing our faith, and in honoring the dignity of every human person.

KNOW, LOVE, AND SERVE

Generations of older Catholics were brought up on the Baltimore Catechism, which instructed them in simple terms on the foundations of their faith. In the very first lesson, we are instructed that God made us "to know Him, to love Him, and to serve Him in this world, and to be happy with Him forever in the next."
How do we do this?

To know God, we must not only attend Mass and receive the sacraments regularly. We need also to pray, to study the Bible, and pursue a regimen of spiritual reading. Saint Isidore of Seville instructs us that "Prayer purifies us, reading instructs us….If a man wants to be always in God's company, he must pray regularly and read regularly. When we pray, we talk to God; when we read, God talks to us."

To love God, we must first keep his Commandments. (John 14:15). We must also spend time with him not only at Mass, but in silent times at home and at Adoration in church. The story is told of an elderly man who regularly sat in an empty church in silence. When the priest asked him what he was doing, he replied that "I talk to God and He talks to me."

To serve God, an excellent starting place is to practice both the corporal and spiritual works of mercy.

CHRIST AS LIGHT

A common metaphor for Christ is to consider Him as Light. In the prologue to John's Gospel, for example, Christ is described as "the light of the human race; the light shines in the darkness, and the darkness has not overcome it."

The Light of Christ is a common theme in the Benedictine tradition. As just one example, Glenstal Abbey in Limerick, Ireland, features the theme of light in its two editions of *The Glenstal Book of Daily Prayer*. Lauds begins with "invocation of the light," with the praise "Glory be to God who has shown us the light!" Vespers often begins with an invocation to "O joyful light of the holy glory of the Immortal Father, heavenly, holy, blessed Jesus Christ!"

Christ Himself declared that "I am the light of the world. Whoever follows me will not walk in darkness, but will have the light of life" (John 8:12) Saint Paul calls on each of us to follow Christ and to "Live as children of light, for light produces every kind of goodness, righteousness and truth." (Ephesians 5:8-9). Indeed, Romans 13:12 describes light as an "armor" which we need to put on.

Sin thrusts us into the depths of darkness. Christ the Light shines in that darkness if we call on Him, and His light will not be overcome. Go to the light always.

AN EXPANDED DOXOLOGY

Glory be to the Father, our Creator who gave us life, Who preserves our life, to reconcile our sinful self to Him,
Who created the vast universe, and the beauty of creation.

Glory be to the Son, our Redeemer, the Son of God, the Word of God,
Who came down from heaven as the Word made flesh,
Who took a human body to share our humanity, so we could share His divinity,
Who was crucified and died on a cross for our sins,
Who rose from the dead, and ascended into heaven,
Who did not abandon us, but left us His body and blood to unite us with Him in heaven.

Glory be to the Holy Spirit, our advocate and guide,
Who offers us the gifts of wisdom, understanding, counsel, fortitude, knowledge, piety, and fear of the Lord.

Glory be to the Father, to the Son, and to the Holy Spirit,
As it was in the beginning, is now, and ever shall be, world without end.

Amen!

ABOUT THE AUTHOR

Edward F. Mannino is a lawyer and historian. He is a Knight of Malta and previously chaired the Education and Defense of the Faith Committee of the Philadelphia Area of the Order of Malta, American Association. He is the author of seven books on Law and on History, including *Faith of Our Fathers: An American Catholic History*.

Mannino has taught as an Adjunct in the History Departments of the University of Pennsylvania and Chestnut Hill College. He has also served as a Commonwealth Trustee of Temple University, and as an Overseer of the College of Arts and Sciences of the University of Pennsylvania.

As a lawyer, he was honored by the *National Law Journal* as one of the "Nation's Top Litigators," and was listed for many years in both *The Best Lawyers in America* and *Chambers USA's America's Leading Lawyers for Business*.

Ed is married to Antoinette ("Toni") O'Connell, a Dame of Malta, and a former training executive on Wall Street. They live in Gwynedd Valley, Pennsylvania.

www.ingramcontent.com/pod-product-compliance
Lightning Source LLC
Chambersburg PA
CBHW020021050426
42450CB00005B/579